SHAYKH AL-SULAMĪ'S WAṢIYYAH

SHAYKH AL-SULAMĪ'S WAṢIYYAH

Practical Spiritual Advice for Muslim Self-Care

Abū 'Abd al-Raḥmān al-Sulamī

Translation & notes by

MUSA FURBER

Last updated: 7 August 2020

ISBN 978-1-944904-17-3 (paper)
978-1-944904-16-6 (EPUB)

Published by:
Islamosaic
islamosaic.com

The COVID-19 edition

Cover image licensed by Ingram Image

بسم الله الرحمن الرحيم

All praise is to Allah alone, the Lord of the Worlds
And may He send His benedictions upon
our master Muhammad, his Kin
and his Companions
and grant them
peace

TRANSLITERATION KEY

ء	ʾ (A distinctive glottal stop made at the bottom of the throat.)
ا	ā, a
ب	b
ت	t
ث	th (Pronounced like the *th* in *think*.)
ج	j
ح	ḥ (Hard *h* sound made at the Adam's apple in the middle of the throat.)
خ	kh (Pronounced like *ch* in Scottish *loch*.)
د	d
ذ	dh (Pronounced like *th* in *this*.)
ر	r (A slightly trilled *r* made behind the upper front teeth.)
ز	z
س	s
ش	sh
ص	ṣ (An emphatic *s* pronounced behind the upper front teeth.)
ض	ḍ (An emphatic *d*-like sound made by pressing the entire tongue against the upper palate.)
ط	ṭ (An emphatic *t* sound produced behind the front teeth.)
ظ	ẓ (An emphatic *th* sound, like the *th* in *this*, made behind the front teeth.)
ع	ʿ (A distinctive Semitic sound made in the middle of the throat and sounding to a Western ear more like a vowel than a consonant.)
غ	gh (A guttural sound made at the top of the throat resembling the untrilled German and French *r*.)
ف	f
ق	q (A hard *k* sound produced at the back of the palate.)
ك	k
ل	l
م	m
ن	n
ه	h (This sound is like the English *h* but has more body. It is made at the very bottom of the throat and pronounced at the beginning, middle, and ends of words.)
و	ū, u
ي	ī, i, y
ﷺ	A supplication made after mention of the Prophet Muḥammad, translated as "May Allah bless him and give him peace."

CONTENTS

PREFACE IX

AUTHOR'S INTRODUCTION 1

1. Be mindful of Allah 2
2. Give priority to obeying Allah and avoiding disobedience 3
3. Do not be distracted from Allah 4
4. Remember, recite, and ponder the Quran 5
5. Follow the Sunna 6
6. Imitate the Righteous Forebears 7
7. Accompany the elite and avoid the wicked 8
8. Do not visit rulers 9
9. Be wary of visiting those who cling to this world 11
10. Have no concern for affairs of this world 12
11. Demand the best from yourself 13
12. Leave what does not concern you 14
13. Be sincere 15
14. Realize truth in your sincerity 16

15. Continually seek forgiveness 17
16. Beware of loving this world 19
17. Accompany those who abstain from this world 20
18. Take from this world only what you must 22
19. Obey and be devoted to your parents 23
20. Maintain familial relations 24
21. Perfect your character 25
22. Honor your neighbors 26
23. Assist all who seek aid 27
24. Accept excuses 28
25. Do not reveal a Muslim's shame 29
26. Counter wickedness with excellence 30
27. Avoid envy 31
28. Respect elders; be clement with the young 32
29. Adhere to modesty 33
30. Be humble with the poor and kind to them 34
31. Keep aloof from the wealthy 35
32. Show compassion towards the pious wealthy 36
33. Seek advice from those who fear their Lord 37

34. Rely upon Allah when you become resolved 38
35. Seek favor with your brothers 39
36. Tell the truth 40
37. Protect your soul and your hearing 41
38. Treat people without prejudice 42
39. Devote yourself to repentance 43
40. Avoid unwholesome food 44
41. Be vigilant of Allah at all times 45
42. Remember Allah continually 46
43. Minimize laughter 47
44. Consider death near 48
45. Give sincere advice 49
46. Rely on Allah for your guidance 50
General counsels 51
Closing counsel 52
REFERENCES 53

PREFACE

This booklet contains the detailed counsel of Imām Abū ʿAbd al-Raḥmān Muḥammad ibn al-Ḥusayn ibn Muḥammad al-Sulamī (325–412 AH/937–1021 CE). Imām Abū ʿAbd al-Raḥmān al-Sulamī authored over one hundred works. He is most famous for his writings related to spiritual development and its masters. However, he was also an accomplished scholar of the Shāfiʿī school of law, a hadith narrator, and a historian.

The shaykh's detailed counsel contains forty-six counsels. Each counsel concerns actions Allah and His Messenger (may Allah bless him and give him peace) have commanded us to perform or avoid. Each of the actions in the counsels impacts one's physical, moral, and spiritual well-being and development. While there is a fair amount of overlap between the content of the shaykh's counsels here and his Infamies of the Soul, the presentation here is lighter. I strongly recommend that anyone who reads these two books spend more time working with the material than they spend reading it. I also recommend that they allocate their time for one to three items each week—skipping items that are not currently applicable.[1]

1. For more recommendations, please see my advice on how to benefit from Infamies of the Soul. "Advice

I first learned about the book when I received a copy from Shaykh Amīn al-Farūqī (may Allah protect him) who had included it in his edition of *ʿUyūb al-nafs* (Infamies of the Soul). His edition was published in Damascus by Dār Maktabat al-Beirūtī repeatedly in the mid-1990s, along with Shaykh Amīn's numerous annotations.

I relied on Shaykh Amīn's edition for my first draft translation, which I then corrected against other editions as I encountered them. I have followed Shaykh Amīn's example in organizing the book into forty-six counsels and for titling each one. The text includes many narrations. Many of these narrations convey information attributed to the Prophet (may Allah bless him and give him peace) and his Companions (may Allah be pleased with them). Others convey information attributed to the Successors, and also from the Pious Forebears (may Allah grant them all His mercy). Many of these narrations are mentioned along with their chains of transmission. These chains and attributions are not always authentic, though the contents of the narrations are accepted. I have tried to track down the earliest source for every narration and quotation in the book, and I advise readers to consult the notes when quoting the book.

Where I have succeeded, it is only through the grace of Allah. Where I have faltered, it is from my

for benefiting from Infamies of the Soul" (https://musafurber.com/2019/12/19/advice-for-benefiting-from-infamies-of-the-soul/).

own shortcomings. May Allah forgive the author, everyone mentioned in the book, its owners, readers, listeners, and all Muslims—living and dead.

MUSA FURBER
PUTRAJAYA
MARCH 25, 2020)

AUTHOR'S INTRODUCTION

This is the counsel of Shaykh Abū ʿAbd al-Raḥmān ibn al-Ḥusayn al-Sulamī, may the Mercy of Allah be upon him. Amīn! Amīn!

In the Name of Allah, the Merciful and Compassionate. May the prayers and blessings of Allah be upon our master Muhammad, and upon his folk and companions.

1

BE MINDFUL OF ALLAH

I counsel you, O brother—may Allah perfect your success—and myself to be mindful of Allah [for] it suffices for every harm. Even if you were to protect yourself from people, it would not free you from needing Allah—not one iota.

Allah Most High says, "And whoever fears Allah, He will appoint a way out for him. And will provide for him from where he did not expect" (Q65:2–3), and "Allah will ease the hardship of he who fears Him" (Q65:4).

2

GIVE PRIORITY TO OBEYING ALLAH AND AVOIDING DISOBEDIENCE

I counsel you: Give priority to obeying Allah Most High and avoiding what contravenes Him. Advance towards Him wholly, return to Him at every worry, and assign it to Him. Cease inclining towards people and relying upon them. Do not dare to turn to them for any of your needs. Instead, your recourse is Allah, and your foundation and reliance are upon Him, for Allah Most High says, "Allah is sufficient for the man who puts his trust in Him" (Q65:3).

It is known that all people lack ability and are managed. How can one incapable of benefiting himself be capable of helping another? Thus, one of the Forebears said, "People seeking aid from people is like prisoners seeking aid from [other] prisoners."[2]

---

2. The author identifies him as Ḥamdūn bin Aḥmed bin ʿAmārah, Abū Ṣālih al-Qassār al-Naysābūrī (d. 271 AH) in his *Tabaqāt al-ṣūfiyyah*, p111, cf p109.

3

DO NOT BE DISTRACTED FROM ALLAH

See that your family, property, or child do not distract you from Allah Most High, lest your entire life be a loss.

Allah Most High says, "O believers! Let neither your riches nor your children divert you from Allah's remembrance. Those who do so, they are the losers" (Q63:9).

4

REMEMBER, RECITE, AND PONDER THE QURAN

You draw nearer to Allah Most High through remembering Him by reading His book—and by pondering, contemplating, and understanding the orders and prohibitions that address you. [Do this, then] comply with His commands and restrain yourself from His prohibitions.

5

FOLLOW THE SUNNA

Follow the Sunna of the Prophet (may Allah bless him and give him peace) in all your words and deeds, and all your material pursuits and states. Dare not contravene the Sunna in what is subtle or what is self-evident. For Allah Most High says, "And let those who conspire to evade orders beware lest an affliction befall them or a painful torment" (Q24:63), and "If you obey him you shall have been guided" (Q24:54).

6

IMITATE THE RIGHTEOUS FOREBEARS

Follow the course of the Righteous Forebears in commanding the right and forbidding the wrong.

Start with yourself in this, for Allah Most High says while telling the story of Shuʿayb (peace be upon him), "I do not wish to do the opposite of what you do and commit that which I forbid you to do" (Q11:88).

And Allah Most High revealed to ʿĪsā (peace be upon him): "Preach to yourself. If you heed your own preaching, then preach to others. Otherwise: be shy from Me."[3]

---

3. Al-Asbahānī, *Hilyat al-awliyā'*, 2:382; Ibn Abī al-Dunyā, *Al-Amr bi-l-maʿrūf wa al-Nahī ʿan al-Munkar,* 97; Aḥmed bin Ḥanbal, *Al-Zuhd,* 300; al-Māwardī, *Adab al-dīn wa-l-dunyā,* 33–34; al-Qushayrī, *Al-Risālah al-Qushayriyyah,* 2:369; al-Ghazālī, *Iḥyā' ʿulūm al-dīn,* 1:63, 2:312, 2:330, 4:416.

7

ACCOMPANY THE ELITE AND AVOID THE WICKED

Habituate yourself with keeping company of the elite, and keeping far from the wicked. It is related that the Prophet (may Allah bless him and give him peace) said, "Whoever resembles a people is one of them."[4]

And he (may Allah bless him and give him peace) said, "Whoever loves a people is one of them."

He [also] (may Allah bless him and give him peace) said, "People are with the ones they love."[5]

And he (may Allah bless him and give him peace) said, "Do not accompany anyone except a believer, and do not feed anyone your food except one who fears Allah."[6]

Abū Turāb al-Nakhshī said, "Keeping company with evil people leads to assuming evil in those who are good."[7]

---

4. Abū Dāwūd, 4031.
5. Al-Bukhārī, 6168–6171; Muslim, 2640 #165.
6. Abū Dāwūd, 4832.
7. Al-Sulamī, *ʿUyūb al-nafs*, 33; *Infamies of the Soul*, p79; al-Māwardī, *Adab al-dīn wa-l-dunyā*, 168.

8

DO NOT VISIT RULERS

Do not dare to visit rulers, stepping across their carpets and assemblies, and becoming familiar with them. The Prophet (may Allah bless him and give him peace) said, "Do not dare to visit them! Whoever believes their lies or aids them in their tyranny: he is not from me, and I am not from him—and he will not drink from the Pool.[8] Whoever visits them and does not believe their lies or help them in their oppression: he is from me, and I am from him—and he will drink from the Pool."[9]

If you must visit them, do not deprive them of sincere advice; and order them to do the right and forbid them the wrong.

It is related that the Prophet (may Allah bless him and give him peace) said, "The best of the martyrs

---

8. The watering trough of the Prophet (may Allah bless him and give him peace) in the Afterlife, from which only the faithful will drink.
9. I could not find a hadith with this same wording. However, some hadiths match this beginning from the phrase "There will be leaders after me: whoever visits them and believes their lies...." See al-Tirmidhī, 2259; al-Nasā'ī, 4208.

is Hamza ibn ʿAbd al-Muṭṭalib and a man who stood up to a tyrant and ordered and forbade."[10]

10. Al-Ājūrī (d360 AH), *al-Sharīʿah,* 5:2245 #1727; al-Khatīb al-Baghdādī, *Tarīkh Baghdād,* 6:374, #3410.

9

BE WARY OF VISITING THOSE WHO CLING TO THIS WORLD

Minimize visiting the comfortable children who cling to this world, since visiting them and looking at their adornments renders Allah's blessings upon you small in your eye. Allah Most High says to His Prophet (may Allah bless him and give him peace), "Do not strain your eyes by looking at [the worldly property] which we have given some of them to enjoy; the splendor of the life of the world, through which We only test them. The provision of your Lord is better and more lasting" (Q20:131).

The Prophet (may Allah bless him and give him peace) said, "Look to him who is below you [in rank] and do not look to him who is above since it is more likely that you fail to notice the blessing of Allah upon you."[11]

11. Narrations with similar wording are in Ibn Mājah, 4142; al-Tirmidhī, 2513.

10

HAVE NO CONCERN FOR AFFAIRS OF THIS WORLD

Do not be concerned with anything from this world. It has been conveyed that Yayhā ibn Muʿādh said, "The world in its entirety does not equal one hour's distress. What, then, of you distressing your entire life in this world, given how little you get from it?"[12]

---

12. Elsewhere, he mentions it as "in its entirety" and "from its beginning to its end." See al-Sulamī, *Adāb al-suḥbah*, 80; *Tabqāt al-ṣūfiyyah*, 99.

11

DEMAND THE BEST FROM YOURSELF

Demand from yourself, at all times, to do whatever is the best for you in that instant. Sahl ibn ʿAbd Allāh said, "Your time is the dearest of things upon you, so occupy it with the dearest of things."[13]

Someone said, "The dearest thing to you is your heart and your time; protect them both."[14]

13. Al-Sulamī, *Al-Futuwwa,* p37.
14. I could not locate this.

12

LEAVE WHAT DOES NOT CONCERN YOU

Leave whatever deeds, utterances, motions, and endeavors that do not concern you. The Prophet (may Allah bless him and give him peace) said, "Part of perfecting a person's Islam is his leaving that which does not concern him."[15]

15. Ibn Mājah, 3976; al-Tirmidhī, 2317-18.

13

BE SINCERE

Maintain sincerity in all works, acts of obedience, and dealings. Allah Most High says, "And they have been ordered no more than this: To worship Allah sincerely, being True [in faith]" (Q98:5).

It is related that the Prophet (may Allah bless him and give him peace) said, "Make your deeds sincere, and a small quantity [of deeds] will suffice you."[16]

---

16. There are several variations of this narration, including: "Make your religion sincere" (Al-Bayhaqī, *Shuʿab al-īmān,* 9:174 #6443, 9:175 #6444); "Be sincere and small quantities of deeds will suffice you" (Al-Ḥakīm al-Tirmidhī, *Nawādir al-uṣūḷ fī aḥādīth al-Rasūl,* 1:91); and "Be sincere [in your religion], and small quantities of deeds will suffice you" (Ibn Mulaqqin, *Mukhtaṣar Talkhīṣ al-Dhahabī,* 6:2944 #993).

14

REALIZE TRUTH IN YOUR SINCERITY

Require your *nafs* to be truthful regarding your sincerity and all of your dealings since each state devoid of truth is dust [in the wind].

Allah Most High says, "Of the believers, there are men who fulfilled what they promised Allah" (Q33:23).

The Prophet (may Allah bless him and give him peace) said, "Truth guides to piety."[17]

---

17. Al-Bukhārī, 6094; Muslim, 2607 #103, 2607 #105. The hadith continues: "...and piety guides to Paradise; lying guides [to immorality, and immorality guides to] the fire."

15

CONTINUALLY SEEK FORGIVENESS

Continually think about your previous violations, since the Prophet (may Allah bless him and give him peace) was continually thinking and always somber.[18]

While pondering, think about your violations and the sins you committed. [Do this,] so they become heavy upon you, and you start to regret, repent, and seek forgiveness. The Prophet (may Allah bless him and give him peace) said, "Regret is repentance."[19]

And he (peace be upon him) said, "Whoever makes plentiful their seeking forgiveness, Allah makes for him an opening from every distress, an exit from every disaster, and sustains him from where he did not expect."[20]

---

18. Ibn Abī al-Dunyā, *Al-Hamm wa-l-ḥuzn,* 2; al-Kharā'iṭī, *I'tilāl al-qulūb,* 7; al-Ṭabarānī, *Musnad al-shāmiyyīn,* 1480, 2012; Ibn 'Adī al-Jurjānī, *Al-Kāmil fī du'afā' al-rijāl,* 2:210; al-Hākim, *Al-Mustadrak,* 7884.
19. Ibn Mājah, 4252.
20. Muhammad bin Naṣr al-Marwazī (294 AH),

He (peace be upon him) said, "The one who repents from sins is the same as one who is sinless."[21]

Mukhtaṣar Qiyām al-layl wa qiyām Ramaḍān wa qiyām al-witr, p98; al-Hākim, 7677. cf Ibn Mājah, 3819.

21. Ibn Mājah, 4250.

16

BEWARE OF LOVING THIS WORLD

Minimize mixing with the sons of this world, since they will propel you to seek it and increase from it, and be preoccupied with it instead of Allah Most High. Allah Most High has forbidden this for you and taught you its condition in His statement (Most High is He): "Know that the life of this world is only playing, and diversion, and adornment, and boasting among you, and rivalry in respect of wealth and children" (Q57:20).

17

ACCOMPANY THOSE WHO ABSTAIN FROM THIS WORLD

You must keep company with those who are abstinent in this world. [You must] mix with the righteous, those who desire the afterlife, and those who leave their portion of this disappearing world [out of] seeking the pleasure of Allah upon them and the afterlife. Allah Most High told of two groups, saying: "Whoever desires the immediate [gains of this world], We hasten him what We will to whom We will, then We appoint for him Hell, which he will endure, disgraced and vanquished. And whoever desires the Hereafter and strives for it as is due to it, being a believer, these will have their striving rewarded" (Q17:18–19).

He made the outcome for those who seek this world—regardless of how they loved it and how they desired it—an eternal rest in the Fire. He made the outcome for those who seek the next world and those who strive for the Hereafter an endeavor worthy of gratitude. This endeavor is excellence in advancing towards Allah, standing in front of Him, and desiring what He has. Allah thanks them for their striving, and He gives them the best of what they request and desire: being near and gazing towards Him. Allah Most High says, "The Allah-fearing are in gardens and rivers. In a seat of truth, near a Powerful King" (Q54:54–55), and He Most High says, "On that day their faces will be radiant, looking at their Lord" (Q75:22–23).

18

TAKE FROM THIS WORLD ONLY WHAT YOU MUST

Minimize [taking] from this world as much as you are able—except for the amount that suffices you—since it preoccupies you from obeying Allah, your Lord.

The Prophet (may Allah bless him and give him peace) said, "All you need from this world [*al-dunyā*] is what satiates your hunger and covers your nakedness. If you have a house that shades you, it suffices you—for bread, water bottled in earthenware, and anything beyond your loincloth counts against you."[22]

22. Al-Ṭabarānī, *Al-Muʿjam al-awsaṭ*, 9343; al-Bayhaqī, *Shuʿab al-īmān*, 9874.

19

OBEY AND BE DEVOTED TO YOUR PARENTS

Obey your parents, for Allah Most High attached their rights with His right. He Most High said, "Thank Me and your two parents. To me is the return" (Q31:14).

The Prophet (may Allah bless him and give him peace) was asked: "To whom must I be most devoted?" He (may Allah bless him and give him peace) said: "Your mother." He asked, "And then?" He (may Allah bless him and give him peace) replied, "Your mother." He asked, "Then whom?" He (may Allah bless him and give him peace) replied, "Your mother." And then it was asked, "Then whom?" He (may Allah bless him and give him peace) replied, "Your father, then your kin [in order of nearness]."[23]

---

23. Al-Tirmidhī, 1897; Abū Dāwūd, 5139–40; Ibn Mājah, 3658.

20

MAINTAIN FAMILIAL RELATIONS

Maintain familial relations, since familial relationships increase throughout [one's] life. Breaking familial ties is among the enormities, since the Prophet (may Allah bless him and give him peace) said, "The womb [*al-raḥim*] is derived from 'the Merciful' [*Al-Raḥmān*]. Allah says: 'Whoever connects you, I connect to him; and whoever breaks you, I break from him.'"[24]

24. Al-Bukhārī, 5988–89; al-Tirmidhī, 1924.

21

PERFECT YOUR CHARACTER

Perfect your character toward your brothers, companions, servants, and your charges. The Prophet (may Allah bless him and give him peace) said to Muʿādh ibn Jabal (may Allah be pleased with him) when delegating him to Yemen, "Perfect your character, O Muʿādh ibn Jabal!"[25]

He (may Allah bless him and give him peace) said, "Good character is the heaviest thing put on the scale [on Judgment Day]."[26]

25. Mālik bin Anas, *Al-Muwaṭṭa'*, 2:902 #1.
26. Al-Tirmidhī, 2002–2003; Abū Dāwūd, 4799.

22

HONOR YOUR NEIGHBORS

Respect your neighbors and be kind to them. The Prophet (may Allah bless him and give him peace) said, "Perfect being neighborly with your neighbors, and you will be a Muslim."[27] And he (may Allah bless him and give him peace) said, "Jibrīl did not cease giving me advice regarding my neighbor until I thought he would inherit from me."[28]

27. Transmissions attribute it being said to Abū Hurayrah and to Abū Dardā' (may Allah be pleased with them). Muḥammad bin Jaʿfar al-Kharā'iṭī (d327 AH), *Makārim al-akhlāq*, p96 #252; and Muḥammad bin Salāmah al-Qaḍā'ī (d454 AH), *Musnad al-Shihāb*, 1:372 #642.
28. Al-Bukhārī, 6015; Muslim, 2625 #141.

23

ASSIST ALL WHO SEEK AID

Assist whoever seeks aid from you, since the Prophet (may Allah bless him and give him peace) said, "Allah aids [His] servant as long as the servant aids his Muslim brother."[29]

29. Muslim, 2699 #38 – though without "brother" being qualified.

24

ACCEPT EXCUSES

Accept an excuse from whoever offers one—whether he is truthful or lying. Allah Most High praised His prophet Yūsuf (may Allah bless him and give him peace) for accepting the excuse of his brothers in His saying, "No reproach, this day, shall be on you. May Allah forgive you, and He is the Most Merciful of the merciful" (Q12:92).

It was related that the Prophet (may Allah bless him and give him peace) said, "Whoever was given an excuse by his Muslim brother and did not accept it, has the same sin upon him as does a tax collector."[30]

30. Al-Sulamī, *Ādāb al-suḥbah,* p100 #145; al-Ghazālī, *Iḥyā' 'ulūm al-dīn*, 2:185. cf Abū Dāwūd, *Al-Marāsīl,* p351 #521.

25

DO NOT REVEAL A MUSLIM'S SHAME

Do not reveal a Muslim's covering [of a sin], since the Prophet (may Allah bless him and give him peace) said, "Whoever veils the shame of his Muslim brother, Allah will veil his shame."[31]

31. Ibn Mājah, 2546.

26

COUNTER WICKEDNESS WITH EXCELLENCE

Counter breaking [family] ties with mending them, wickedness with excellence, and tyranny with patience and forgiveness. The Prophet (may Allah bless him and give him peace) said, "Mend family ties with whoever breaks them, excuse whoever oppressed you, show excellence to whoever is evil towards you."[32]

32. Several hadiths mention two of the three things referred to in this hadith. cf Ibn Abi al-Dunyā, *Makārim al-akhlāq*, #20; al-Bayhaqī, *Shuʿab al-īmān*, 7585, 7723, 7725.

27

AVOID ENVY

Avoid envy concerning matters related to this world. The Prophet (may Allah bless him and give him peace) said, "Do not envy one another."[33]

33. Al-Bukhārī, 6064–66, 6076; Muslim, 2558 #23, 2559 #24, 2563 #28, 2563 #30, 2564 #32.

28

RESPECT ELDERS; BE CLEMENT WITH THE YOUNG

Respect elders and be merciful towards the young. The Prophet (may Allah bless him and give him peace) said, "Whoever did not show mercy towards our young and did not respect our elders is not one of us."[34]

34. Al-Bukhārī, *Al-Adab al-mufrad,* 358; al-Tirmidhī, 1919–21.

29

ADHERE TO MODESTY

Adhere to modesty. The Prophet (may Allah bless him and give him peace) said, "Modesty is a part of belief,"[35] and he (may Allah bless him and give him peace) said, "All modesty is good."[36]

35. Al-Bukhārī, 24, 6118; Muslim, 36 #59.
36. Muslim, 37 #60.

30

BE HUMBLE WITH THE POOR AND KIND TO THEM

Be humble with the poor, pity them, and be kind to them. Allah Most High admonished His Messenger (may Allah bless him and give him peace), and He Most High said, "Send not away those who call upon their Lord at morning and evening, seeking only His Face" (Q6:52).

31

KEEP ALOOF FROM THE WEALTHY

Keep aloof from the wealthy. Sufyān al-Thawrī said, "Aloofness towards the wealthy causes rights to reach their owners and those who deserve them."

32

SHOW COMPASSION TOWARDS THE PIOUS WEALTHY

Show compassion towards the wealthy who feel sufficiency is from their Lord and not from any of this world's trinkets. It was related that the Prophet (may Allah bless him and give him peace) said, "The wealthy who are thankful have the same rewards as the poor who are patient."[37]

37. I could not locate a hadith or narration with this wording.

33

SEEK ADVICE FROM THOSE WHO FEAR THEIR LORD

Seek advice in your affairs from those who fear their Lord at night [when there is no one to see them] and those who fear Allah through [following] his religion and his safe-keeping. Allah Most High says to His Prophet (may Allah bless him and give him peace), "and consult with them in the conduct of [communal] affairs" (Q3:159).

34

RELY UPON ALLAH WHEN YOU BECOME RESOLVED

If you become resolved to do something after receiving counsel, put your reliance upon Allah solely, and sever your association with the created world. Allah Most High says, "and when you are resolved, put your trust in Allah" (Q3:159).

Relying upon Allah is entrusting all of your affairs to Allah the Exalted and Most High in whole, and being content with the excellence of His choices for you and His planning.

35

SEEK FAVOR WITH YOUR BROTHERS

Seek favor with your brothers and companions by helping and serving them and being kind towards them. It was related that the Prophet (may Allah bless him and give him peace) said, "Be kind to whoever deserves it and to who does not deserve it. [Even] if he did not deserve it, you did."[38]

The Prophet (may Allah bless him and give him peace) said, "Kindness enters nothing without beautifying it. Stupidity enters nothing without disgracing it."[39]

---

38. Al-Bazzār, Muḥammad bin ʿAbd Allāh (d354 AH), *Kitāb al-fawāʾid* ("*Al-Ghaylāniyāt*"), 78; al-Sulamī, *Ādāb al-suḥbah*, 138; al-Ghazālī, *Iḥyāʾ ʿulūm al-dīn,* 2:196, 3:245; al-ʿIrāqī, *Takhrīj aḥādīth Iḥyāʾ ʿulūm al-dīn,* 1695 (weak).
39. I could not locate this specific wording. A narration with similar wording is found in Muslim, 2594 #78.

36

TELL THE TRUTH

Habituate your tongue to the truth, uttering what is good, and speaking it. The Prophet (may Allah bless him and give him peace) said, "And are people thrown down on their nostrils in the Hellfire except by what their tongues reap?"[40]

Abū Bakr al-Siddīq (Allah be well pleased with him) grasped his tongue to advise it, and began saying: "This thing has brought me to the brink of catastrophe."[41]

---

40. Ibn Jārūd al-Ṭayālisī, *Musnad Abī Dāwūd al-Ṭayālisī,* 561; Ibn Abī Shaybah, *Al-Muṣannaf,* 26498; Aḥmed bin Ḥanbal, *Al-Musnad,* 22063, 22068; al-Bazzār, *Musnad* ("*Al-Bahr al-zakhkhār*"), 2302, 2643; al-Māwardī, *Adab al-dīn wa al-dunyā,* 278.

41. Ibn Wahb (d197 AH), *Al-Jāmiʿ fi-l-ḥadīth,* 307; al-Bazzār, *Musnad* ("*Al-Bahr al-zakhkhār*"), 84; al-Bayhaqī, *Shuʿab al-īmān,* 4596, 8890.

37

PROTECT YOUR SOUL AND YOUR HEARING

Protect your soul and your hearing from listening to lies, slander, false accusations, and excesses. Allah Most High says, "for [man's] eyes, ears and heart, each of these shall be questioned about this" (Q17:36).

The Prophet (may Allah bless him and give him peace) said, "The listener is the speaker's accomplice."[42]

42. Attributed to the Prophet (may Allah bless him and give him peace): al-Sulamī, *Ādāb al-ṣuḥbah,* 158; al-Ghazālī, *Iḥyāʾ ʿulūm al-dīn,* 2:336; cf al-ʿIrāqī, *Takhrīj aḥādīth Iḥyāʾ ʿulūm al-dīn,* 278, 813.
Attributed to Imam al-Shāfiʿī: al-Asbahānī, Abū Naʿīm Aḥmad, *Ḥilyāt al-awliyā wa ṭabaqāt al-aṣfiyāʾ*, 9:123; al-Ghazālī, *Iḥyāʾ ʿulūm al-dīn,* 1:25.
Attributed to an unnamed individual: Ibn Abī al-Dunyā, *Al-Ṣamt,* 247; Ibn Abī al-Dunyā, *Dhamm al-ghībah wa-l-namīmah,* 111.

38

TREAT PEOPLE WITHOUT PREJUDICE

Do not treat people with prejudice, yet do not demand that they treat you without prejudice. It is related that the Prophet (may Allah bless him and give him peace) said, "The noblest of deeds is the remembrance of Allah Mighty and Magnificent, and treating people without prejudice from yourself."[43]

43. Al-Sulamī, *Ādāb al-suḥbah*, 172.

39

DEVOTE YOURSELF TO REPENTANCE

Devote yourself to repentance during every moment [in which] you are alone. The Prophet (may Allah bless him and give him peace) said, "Indeed, I repent to Allah each day one hundred times."[44]

---

44. With a slight variation in wording: Muslim, 2702 #42.

40

AVOID UNWHOLESOME FOOD

Avoid eating anything unlawful or questionable. [Avoid] the food of immoral individuals and sitting at their table-spreads. Especially [avoid] the property of the ruler and his employees. The Prophet (may Allah bless him and give him peace) said, "All flesh sprouting from ill-gotten gains: the fire is more appropriate for it."[45]

The Prophet (may Allah bless him and give him peace) forbade answering [invitations to eat] the food of the corrupt.[46]

---

45. With a slight variation in wording: al-Hākim, *Al-Mustadrak,* 7164; al-Bayhaqī, *Shuʿab al-īmān,* 5130.
46. Al-Ṭabarānī, *Al-Muʿjam al-awsaṭ,* 441; al-Tabarānī, *Al-Muʿjam al-kabīr,* 376; al-Bayhaqī, *Shuʿab al-īmān,* 5420.

41

BE VIGILANT OF ALLAH AT ALL TIMES

Be vigilant of Allah Most High when you are alone, while performing deeds, and throughout [all] your states. Allah Most High says, "Allah is Watching over you" (Q4:1).

42

REMEMBER ALLAH CONTINUALLY

Be constant in the remembrance of Allah Most High. Through your remembrance of Him, you bring about His remembrance of you. Allah Most High says, "Remember Me, and I will remember you" (Q2:152).

The Prophet (may Allah bless him and give him peace) said that Allah Most High says: "Whomever the Quran and My remembrance preoccupy him from beseeching Me, I give [him] the best of what the beseechers are given."[47]

47. Ibn Abī al-Shaybah, *Muṣannaf,* 29271, 29273; al-Asfahānī, *Ḥilyat al-awliyā',* 7:313; al-Bayhaqī, *Shu'ab al-īmān,* 567–69, 3786.

43

MINIMIZE LAUGHTER

Minimize laughter. It was related that the Prophet (may Allah bless him and give him peace) said, "Much laughter kills the heart."[48]

48. Ibn Mājah, 4193, 4217; al-Tirmidhī, 2305 – *gharīb*.

44

CONSIDER DEATH NEAR

Consider your death near and consider your hopes to be impossible since this will aid you in performing good deeds. It was conveyed that Junayd said, "Whoever is nonexistent in both extents [beginning and end, i.e., before birth and after death], will pass away."[49] Allah Most High said, "Leave them to eat and enjoy themselves and be distracted by hope; for they will come to know" (Q15:3).

The Prophet (may Allah bless him and give him peace) drew two lines and said, "This is the Son of Ādam. This is his life. And these are his hopes."[50]

---

49. I could not find a source for this. The translation follows Shaykh Muḥammad Amīn al-Fārūqī's notes.
50. Al-Bukhāri, 6417. This is part of a longer hadith. Ibn Masʿūd said: "The Prophet (may Allah bless him and give him peace) drew a rectangle. He drew a line in the middle exiting [the rectangle]. He drew short lines toward the line in the middle from the side that is in the middle. Then he said, "This is a man. This is his life encompassing him. The [line] that exits [the rectangle] is his hope. These small lines are the things he found beneficial. When he crosses this one, it stings him, and when he crosses this one, it stings him."

45

GIVE SINCERE ADVICE

Frequently offer sincere advice to people. Jarīr ibn 'Abd Allāh (Allah be well pleased with them both) said, "I pledged allegiance to the Prophet (may Allah bless him and give him peace) to give good counsel to every Muslim."[51]

51. Muslim, 56 #98. cf al-Bukhārī, 2714.

46

RELY ON ALLAH FOR YOUR GUIDANCE

Know that you will not reach any of what I mentioned except through success from Allah, Exalted and Most High.

GENERAL COUNSELS

Always [do the following]:

- struggle
- eat [only what is] lawful
- lower your gaze from what is unlawful and questionable
- protect your tongue from the questionable
- vigilantly monitor your heart
- pay attention to your conscience
- have compassion for people
- offer them sincere counsel
- seek protection from Allah Exalted and Most High frequently
- beseech Allah Most High that He grant you these stations
- impeach your self
- assume the worst when it comes to yourself
- assume the best when it comes to other people
- love the friends of Allah Exalted and Most High because of His love for them
- be kind towards the poor

And whatever follows in the steps of these beautiful behaviors.

CLOSING COUNSEL

Know, O my brother—and may Allah ennoble you with His obedience—that I have offered you this advice even though no one is known to be more negligent in them than me. The person closest to the place of distress is one who preaches but does not himself take heed and is [not] satisfied with what is good. I ask Allah Most High for His remembrance, that He remove from us the seal of heedlessness, and unveil us from the veil of assumptions.

So, I advise you—may Allah consign you to His custody—to pray for me, that I have repentance, so perhaps Allah Most High will be generous with me with it as a bestowal. Indeed, He possesses this and has the ability to do it. May the prayers of Allah be upon our Master Muhammad, and upon his folk and Companions. There is no change and no power except by Allah Most High, Most Great.

All praise belongs to Allah, Lord of the worlds. *Āmīn*. Finished.

REFERENCES

ʿAbd al-Karīm bin Hawāzin bin ʿAbd al-Malik al-Qushayrī (465 AH). *Al-Risālat al-Qushayriyyah.* Edited by ʿAbd al-Ḥalīm Maḥmūd and Maḥmūd bin al-Sharīf. Cairo: Dār al-Maʿārif.

Abū Aḥmed bin ʿAdī al-Jurjānī (365 AH). *Al-Kāmil fī ḍuʿafāʾ al-rijāl.* Edited by ʿĀdil Aḥmed ʿAbd al-Mawjūd, ʿAlī Muḥammad Muʿawwaḍ, and ʿAbd al-Fattāḥ Abū Sunnah. Beirut: Al-Kutub al-ʿIlmiyyah, 1997/1418.

Abū Dāwūd, Sulaymān ibn al-Ashʿath al-Sijistānī. *Sunan Abī Dāwūd.* Edited by Muḥammad Muḥyī al-Dīn ʿAbd al-Ḥamīd. 4 vols. Beirut: al-Maṭbaʿah al-ʿAṣriyyah, n.d.

Abū al-Faḍl Zayn al-Dīn ʿAbd al-Raḥīm al-ʿIrāqī (806 AH). *Al-Mughnī ʿan ḥaml al-asfār fī al-asfār fī takhrīj mā fī Al-Iḥyāʾ min al-akhbār.* Beirut: Dār Ibn Ḥazm, 2005/1426.

Abū Bakr Aḥmed bin ʿAlī bin Thābit bin Aḥmed bin Mahdī (463 AH). *Tārīkh Baghdād*. Edited by Bashshār ʿAwwād Maʿrūf. Beirut: Dār al-Gharb al-Islāmī, 2002/1422.
Abū Bakr bin Abī Shaybah (235 AH). *Al-Kitāb al-Muṣannaf fī al-aḥādīth wa al-āthār.* Edited by Kamāl Yūsuf al-Ḥūt. Riyadh: Maktabat al-Rushd, 1409.
Abū Bakr Muḥammad bin Jaʿfar al-Kharāʾiṭī (327 AH). *Iʿtilāl al-qulūb*. Edited by Ḥamdī al-Damardāsh. Riyadh: Maktabah al-Mukarammah, 2000/1421.
———. *Makārim al-akhlāq*. Edited by Ayman ʿAbd al-Jābir al-Buḥayrī. Cairo: Dār al-Āfāq al-ʿArabiyyah, 1999/1419.
Abū Bakr ʿAbd Allāh bin Muḥammad bin ʿUbayd bin Sufyān ("Ibn Abī al-Dunyā") (281 AH). *Al-Amr bi-l-maʿrūf wa al-nahī ʿan al-munkar.* Edited by Ṣalāḥ bin ʿIyāḍ al-Shalāḥī. n.a.: Maktabat al-Ghurabāʾ al-Athariyyah, 1997/1418.
———. *Al-Ṣamt wa adab al-lisān*. Edited by Abū Isḥāq al-Ḥuwaynī. Beirut: Dār al-Kutub al-ʿIlmiyyah, 1410.
———. *Dhamm al-ghībah wa al-namīmah*. Edited by Bashīr Muḥammad ʿUyūn. Damascus: Dār al-Bayān, 1992/1413.
———. *Al-Hamm wa-l-ḥuzn*. Edited by Majdī al-Sayyid Ibrāhīm. Cairo: Dār al-Salām, 1991/1412,

———. *Makārim al-akhlāq*. Edited by Majdī al-Sayyid Ibrāhīm. Cairo: Maktabat al-Qur'ān, n.d.

Abū Na'īm Aḥmed bin 'Abd Allāh bin Aḥmed al-Aṣbahānī (430AH). *Ḥilyat al-awliyā' wa ṭabaqāt al-aṣfiyā'*. Al-Sa'ādah, 1974/1394.

al-Ājūrī, Abū Bakr Muḥammad bin al-Ḥusein ibn 'Abd Allāh, al-Baghdādī (360AH). *Al-Sharī'ah*. Edited by 'Abd Allāh bin 'Umar bin Sulaymān. Riyadh: Dār al-Waṭn, 1999/1420.

al-Bayhaqī, Aḥmed bin al-Ḥussein bin 'Alī bin Mūsā (458 AH). *Shu'ab al-īmān*. Edited by 'Adb al-'Alī 'Abd al-Ḥamīd Ḥāmid. n.a: Maktabat al-Rushd, 2003/1423.

al-Bazzār, Abū Bakr Muḥammad bin 'Abd Allāh (354 AH). *Kitāb al-fawā'id* ("Al-Ghaylāniyāt"). Edited by Ḥilmī Kāmil As'ad 'Abd al-Hādī. Riyadh: Dār Ibn al-Jawzī, 1997/1417.

al-Bazzār, Abū Bakr Aḥmad bin 'Amr (292 AH). *Musnad al-Bazzār* ("*Al-Baḥr al-zakhkhār*"). Medina: Maktabat al-'Ulūm wa al-Ḥikam, 1988–2009.

al-Bukhārī, Muḥammad bin Ismā'īl bin Ibrāhīm (256 AH). *Al-Adab al-mufrad*. Edited by Muḥammad Fu'ād 'Abd al-Bāqī. Beirut: Dār al-Bashā'ir al-Islāmiyyah, 1989/1409.

———. *Al-Jāmiʿ al-ṣaḥīḥ al-mukhtaṣar.* Edited by Muṣṭafā al-Bughā. Beirut: Dār Ibn Kathīr, 1407/1987.

al-Ghazālī, Abū Ḥāmid Muḥammad bin Muḥammad (505 AH). *Iḥyāʾ ʿulūm al-dīn.* Beirut: Dār al-Maʿrifah, n.d.

al-Ḥakīm al-Tirmidhī, Muḥammad bin ʿAlī (320 AH). *Nawādir al-uṣūl fī aḥādīth al-Rasūl* ﷺ. Edited by ʿAbd al-Raḥmān ʿUmayrah. Beirut: Dār al-Jīl, n.d.

al-Ḥākim, Abū ʿAbd Allāh Muḥammad bin ʿAbd Allāh (405 AH). *Al-Mustadrak ʿalā al-ṣaḥīḥayn.* Edited by Muṣṭafā ʿAbd al-Qādir ʿAṭāʾ. Beirut: Dār al-Kutub al-ʿIlmiyyah, 1990/1411.

al-ʿIrāqi (806 AH), Ibn al-Subkī (771 AH), al-Zabīdī (1205 AH). *Takhrīj aḥādīth Iḥyā ʿulūm al-dīn.* Riyādh: Dār al-ʿĀṣimah li-l-Nashr, 1987/1408.

Ibn Ḥanbal, Abū ʿAbd Allāh Aḥmed bin Muḥammad (241 AH). *Musnad al-Imām Aḥmed bin Ḥanbal.* Edited by Shuʿayb al-Arnāʾūṭ, et al. Beirut: Muʾassisat al-Risālah, 2001/1421.

———. *Al-Zuhd.* Annotated by Muḥammad ʿAbd al-Salām Shāhīn. Beirut: Dār al-Kutub al-ʿIlmiyyah, 1999/1420.

Ibn Mājah (273 AH), Muḥammad. *Sunan Ibn Mājah.* Edited by Fu'ād 'Abd al-Bāqī. 2 vols. Beirut: Dār al-Fikr, n.d.

Ibn Mulaqqin Sirāj al-Dīn Abū Ḥafṣ ʿUmar bin ʿAlī bin Aḥmed al-Shāfiʿī (804 AH). *Mukhtaṣar talkhīṣ al-Dhahabī*. Riyadh: Dār al-ʿĀṣimah, 1411.
Ibn Wahb, Abū Muḥammad (197 AH). *Al-Jāmiʿ fi-l-ḥadīth*. Riyadh: Dār Ibn al-Jawzī, 1995/1416.
al-Khaṭīb al-Baghdādī. *Tarīkh Baghdād*. Edited by Muṣṭafā ʿAbd al-Qādir ʿAṭā. Beirut: Dār al-Kutub al-ʿIlmiyyah, 1417.
Mālik bin Anas (179 AH). *Muwaṭṭaʾ al-Imām Mālik*. Edited by Muḥammad Fuʾād ʿAbd al-Bāqī. Beirut: Lebanon, 1985/1406.
al-Marwazī, Abū ʿAbd Allāh Muḥammad bin Naṣr (294 AH). *Mukhtaṣar Qiyām al-layl wa Qiyām Ramaḍān wa Qiyām al-witr*. Abridged by Aḥmad bin ʿAlī al-Maqrīzī. Faisalabad: Ḥadīth Akādamī, 1988/1408.
al-Māwardī, Abū al-Ḥasan (450 AH). *Adab al-dunyā wa-l-dīn*. Dār Maktabat al-Ḥayāt, 1986.
Muḥammad bin al-Ḥussein bin Muḥammad bin Mūsā bin Khālid bin Sālim al-Naysabūri, Abū ʿAbd al-Raḥmān al-Sulamī (412 AH). *Al-Futuwwah*. Edited by Iḥsān Dhanūn al-Thāmirī and Muḥammad ʿAbd Allāh al-Qadḥāt. Amman: Dār al-Rāzī, 2002/1422.

———. *Ādāb al-ṣuḥbah*. Edited by Majd Fatḥī al-Sayyid. Ṭanṭā: Dār al-Ṣaḥābah li-l-Turāth, 1990/1410.

———. *Ṭabaqāt al-ṣūfiyyah*. Edited by Muṣṭafā ʿAbd al-Qādir ʿAṭā. Beirut: Dār al-Kutub al-ʿIlmiyyah, 1998/1419.

———. *Waṣiyyat al-Sheikh al-Sulamī*. Edited by Majdī Fatḥī al-Sayyid. Tanta: Maktabah al-Ṣaḥābah, n.d.

———. *ʿUyūb al-nafs wa adwiyatuhā*. Edited by Muḥammad Anīn al-Fārūqī. Damascus: Maktabat Dār al-Beiruti, 2003/1424.

———. *Infamies of the Soul and Their Treatments*. Translated by Steven (Musa) Furber. Islamosaic, 2018.

Muslim ibn al-Ḥajjaj (261 AH). *Ṣaḥīḥ Muslim*. Edited by Muḥammad Fu'ād 'Abd al-Bāqī. 5 vols. Cairo: Maṭba'a 'Isā al-Bābī al-Ḥalabī 1376/1956. Reprint. Beirut: Dār al-Fikr, 1403/1983.

al-Nasā'ī, Abū 'Abd al-Raḥmān Aḥmad (303 AH). *Al-Sunan al-Kubrā*. Beirut: Dār Iḥyā' al-Turāth al-'Arabī, n.d.

al-Quḍāʿī, Abū ʿAbd Allāh Muḥammad bin Salāmah bin Jaʿfar bin ʿAlī (454 AH). *Musnad al-Shihāb*. Edited by Ḥamdi bin ʿAbd al-Majīd al-Salafī. Beirut: Muʾassisah al-Risālah, 1986/1407.

Sulaymān bin Aḥmed bin Ayūb bin Muṭīr al-Lakhmī, Abū Qāsim al-Ṭabarānī (360 AH). *Al-Muʿjam al-awsaṭ.* Edited by Ṭāriq bin ʿIwaḍ Allāh bin Muḥammad and ʿAbd al-Muḥsin bin Ibrāhīm al-Ḥusayni. Cairo: Dār al-Ḥaraman, n.d.

———. *Al-Muʿjam al-kabīr.* Edited by Ḥamdī bin ʿAbd al-Majīd. Cairo: Maktabat Dār Ibn Taymiyyah, n.d.

———. *Musnad al-shāmiyyīn.* Edited by Ḥamdī bin ʿAbd al-Majīd al-Salafī. Beirut: Mu'ssisah al-Risālah, 1984/1405.

al-Ṭayālisī, Abū Dāwūd Sulaymān bin Dāwūd bin al-Jārūd (204 AH). *Musnad Abī Dāwūd al-Ṭayālisī.* Edited by Muḥammad bin ʿAbd al-Muḥsin al-Turkī. Egypt: Dār Hijr, 1999/1419.

al-Tirmidhī, Muḥammad ibn ʿĪsā (279 AH). *Sunan al-Tirmidhī.* Edited by Aḥmad Muḥammad Shākir, Muḥammad Fu'ād ʿAbd al-Bāqī, and Ibrāhīm ʿAṭwah ʿAwaḍ. 5 vols. Cairo: al-Bābī al-Ḥalabī, n.d.

Also from Islamosaic

Connecting to the Quran
Etiquette with the Quran
Infamies of the Soul
Hadith Nomenclature Primers
Hanbali Acts of Worship
Ibn Juzay's Sufic Exegesis
Refutation of Those Who Do Not Follow the Four Schools
Sharḥ Al-Waraqāt
Shaykh al-Sulamī's Waṣiyyah
Supplement for the Seeker of Certitude
The Accessible Conspectus
The Encompassing Epistle
The Evident Memorandum
The Ultimate Conspectus

ISLAMOSAIC

www.islamosaic.com